Greek Island Myths

SANTORINI (THIRA)
THE LOST ISLAND OF ATLANTIS

JILL DUDLEY

PUT IT IN YOUR POCKET SERIES
ORPINGTON PUBLISHERS

Published by
Orpington Publishers

Cover design and origination by
Creeds, Bridport, Dorset
01308 423411

Printed and bound in the UK by
Creeds

© Jill Dudley 2016

ISBN: 978-0-9935378-1-3

SANTORINI (THIRA)
THE LOST ISLAND OF ATLANTIS

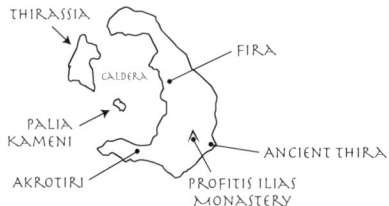

Santorini, or Thira as it is sometimes called, is the southernmost of the Cycladic islands, and one of the most beautiful in the Aegean. It is of grey-black volcanic rock, and its capital Fira with its dazzlingly white houses and domed churches is picturesque as it clings to the cliff-face, which itself plunges nearly two hundred and ten metres down to the port and the glittering blue sea.

In the small port schooners and small boats line the quayside waiting to take passengers around the caldera. The caldera is where Santorini, once a round island (it was earlier called Strangyle, round island) sank in on itself in the volcanic eruption c.1450 B.C., leaving the smaller islands which can be seen around the western circumference.

Mule trains in colourful trappings carry visitors from the

port, mounting shallow steps which zigzag up the steep cliff-face. The steps are constructed in ash-coloured and volcanic-black cobblestones, each one edged with white marble. For those unable to ride a mule there is a cable-car. In the town the narrow, irregular houses are linked by cobbled streets and numerous steps

When the Olympian gods began to filter into the minds of the ancient Greeks, they conjured up the imaginative belief that at first there was only Chaos. In Greek mythology the earth and the heavens created themselves, and in due course Gaea (earth) became personified as the daughter of Chaos; she married Ouranos (the heavens) and gave birth to the Titans and Cyclopes. One of the Titans, Kronos, (whose name means Time) had three sons, Zeus (who became the supreme god of the Olympians), Poseidon, god of the sea, and Hades whose kingdom was the underworld.

It was Plato in the fifth century B.C. who referred to Santorini as being the lost island of Atlantis. In his *Critias* it is suggested that the violent volcanic eruption on Santorini was caused by the severe displeasure of Poseidon, who was not only god of the sea but of earthquakes also, and was often referred to as the 'earth shaker'. According to Plato, when the Olympian gods first came into existence, they portioned out their world amongst themselves, and Poseidon was given the sea together with Atlantis (Santorini).

Poseidon had then divided the island between his five sets of twin sons, and each ruled his share with great success; in other words everyone became wealthy, and were generous and content – as Plato put it, they were 'truehearted' and 'greathearted'. But after some years of such contentment, their endless comfort and luxury became monotonous, so over the years they became less and less 'truehearted' and 'greathearted'. In short, they became fractious, disgruntled and aggressive, till Poseidon could bear them no longer and, with a flick of the hand, he sank the island drowning them all along with it.

Akrotiri, in the south-west of the island, is an archaeological Aladdin's cave of what life was like before that catastrophic eruption. It was a civilization at the height of its power, and the people had acquired a highly advanced life-style. Before the disaster (the late Minoan period c.1450 B.C.) it bore signs of Cretan and Egyptian influence, though some scholars say it was Crete* and Egypt who were influenced by the Akrotirians.

The rich upper classes of Akrotiri lived in two- or three-storey houses, and the walls of their rooms were decorated with fine frescoes, some of which are still in a good state of preservation and can be seen in the Prehistoric Museum in Fira. No human remains have been discovered, however, suggesting that the inhabitants were able to flee before the disaster struck.

It is thought that the citizens of Akrotiri were governed by priests, though excavations have found no temples there. Traces, however, of animal sacrifice such as pigs, sheep and goats (which only the wealthy could have afforded) have been detected. When fleeing the island, the citizens left behind a small gold ibex which they carefully wrapped and placed in a box. It is believed it was left as an offering to the gods to appease their wrath. That too can be seen in the Fira museum.

Santorini is now crescent-shaped. Interestingly, though, from Fira looking out to sea, several islands can be seen which were once part of it, making it easy to detect how it was once a round island. The one now known as Nea Kameni, however, did not rise from the sea until 1707. A Jesuit priest gave a frightening eye-witness account of its first appearance. He described how one morning, where there had been only sea, a protrusion appeared on the sea's surface. Thinking it to be a shipwreck, a few men rowed out to investigate then, finding it was a tiny islet, they secured their boat and climbed on to it. Much to their alarm it began to move and tremble under their feet, so they hastily returned to their boat. Over the next days they watched it sink, then rise and swell. Eventually a huge rock emerged and rose to a height of fifteen metres. The sea meanwhile had been changing colour ceaselessly from bright green to red, to yellow, with an 'oppressive odour' rising from the sea.

The Jesuit wrote a month by month account, describing various small islands appearing, joining then separating and sinking. Smoke was seen from one of the new islets, then flames rising from the smoke. It took five years before the islets finally united and settled down to become the one island now known as Nea Kameni. Today visitors can visit it and walk over the ash-strewn black lava pathway to see the several shallow craters where the whiff of sulphur rises from the ground. The shores of this island are strewn with huge shiny black rocks like monster lumps of coal. On the far side of Nea Kameni can be seen Aspronisi, the colour and shape of a scone. Seismologists keep a continuous check to make sure volcanic activity does not pose a threat. Visitors who would like to swim are given the opportunity to dive overboard into the warm thermal springs at the nearby island of Palia Kameni. The colour of the sea here is in bands of cobalt, emerald, olive green, and sulphur.

Sailing back to the port of Fira on Santorini, you see the huddle of white houses clinging to the grey-black rockface again. Then the train of mules come into focus ascending and descending the zigzagging stepped pathway; and a little way further along the bubbles of the cable cars rising through the air. The beauty of Santorini is breathtaking.

According to the fifth century B.C. historian Herodotus in his *Histories,* a Spartan named Theras, dissatisfied with his life in Sparta, had sailed to Santorini and settled there. The story was that in Sparta Theras had held the all-important position of Regent while his two nephews, destined to become monarchs, had been minors. Once they had become old enough for their royal duties Theras, no longer the ruler, could not stand being a subject, so sailed to the island (at the time called Kalliste, most beautiful) because he had heard that his forebear, the legendary King Cadmus, had visited it, and had liked it so much that he had settled some of his kinsmen on it. As soon as Theras arrived he was spellbound and pronounced himself king, which is why, in his honour, the island was renamed Thira, by which it is often called today. Its ancient capital was also called Thira and is now an archaeological site to the east of the island.

So are the inhabitants of Santorini today 'truehearted' and 'greathearted' as they once were in antiquity? Fortunately, whatever they are, Poseidon the earth-shaker is no longer around to vent his anger. His power over mankind has been outsmarted by men themselves with their scientific instruments which warn them of any impending calamity.

Meanwhile, the gold ibex left behind by the Akrotirians, and the frescoes from the walls of their houses, have been rescued from the devastation of Poseidon's anger. The fresco of the blue monkeys cavorting, and another of a blue monkey gathering saffron from crocuses and giving it to a seated goddess, are to be seen in the museum. Blue monkeys were believed to have religious symbolism; they were once regarded as intermediaries between the world of men and the gods. Maybe it was these monkeys who betrayed to Poseidon that the people of Santorini were no longer 'truehearted' and 'greathearted', thus bringing down the god's wrath. The answer will never be known, but at least the island is re-inhabited, and the islanders themselves welcome the visitor who, when he departs, will leave with an indelible memory imprinted on his mind of a truly beautiful and magical island.

Denotes a separate booklet on the subject.

FAMILY TREE OF THE GODS AND GODDESSES

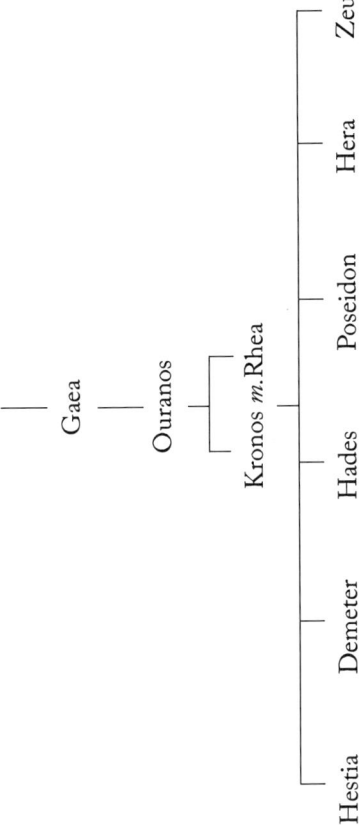

FAMILY TREE OF THE GODS AND GODDESSES

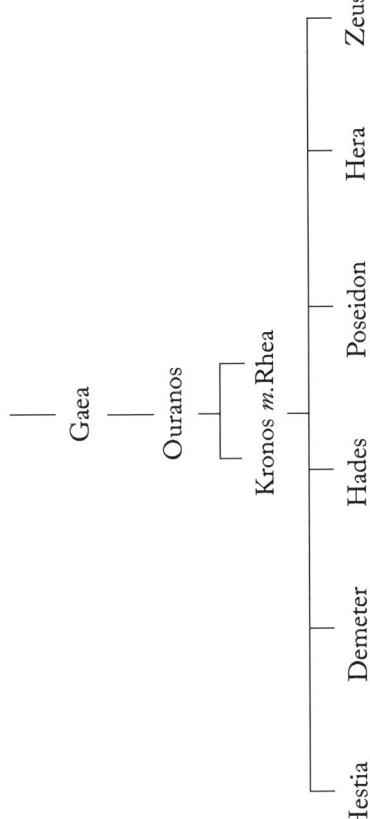

GLOSSARY OF GODS AND GODDESSES

CHAOS – Primordial Chaos from which came Ouranos (the heavens) and Gaea.

GAEA – The personification of the earth, who sprang from Chaos.

KRONOS – A Titan, married to Rhea who gave birth to many of the Olympian gods, including Poseidon and Zeus. His name means Time.

POSEIDON – God of the sea and earthquakes. Brother of Zeus, and often referred to as the 'earth-shaker'. He was the son of Rhea and Kronos.

RHEA – A Titaness, and wife of Kronos. She was mother of Zeus and Poseidon, and other of the Olympian gods.

TITANS – The offspring of Ouranos (the heavens) and Gaea (the earth). There were said to be twelve of them, six sons and six daughters. Kronos was one of the sons, and Rhea one of the daughters. These two gave birth to Poseidon, Zeus and several other of the Olympian gods.

ZEUS – Son of Kronos and Rhea. God of the heavens, and supreme god of the ancient world having deposed his father.

MORE FROM THE
PUT IT IN YOUR POCKET SERIES
GREEK MYTHS

TROJAN WAR
THE JUDGEMENT OF PARIS
HELEN
KING AGAMEMNON
ACHILLES
THE WOODEN HORSE
ODYSSEUS

SACRED SITES
ATHENS – THE ACROPOLIS
CORINTH – ST. PAUL AND THE GODDESS OF LOVE
DELPHI – THE ORACLE OF APOLLO
ELEUSIS – DEMETER AND KORE
EPIDAURUS – CENTRE OF HEALING
OLYMPIA – THE OLYMPIC GAMES

ALSO BY JILL DUDLEY

YE GODS! (TRAVELS IN GREECE)

YE GODS! II (MORE TRAVELS IN GREECE)

LAP OF THE GODS (TRAVELS IN CRETE
AND THE AEGEAN ISLANDS)